Jim Swim

This is Jim.

This is Jim's dad.

This is Jim's mum.
Jim got his skills from her.

Jim can swim as quick as a fish!

If you need help,
just tell me!
Peck!
Snap!

The ship is sinking!

Jim swims to the ship.
Flip!
Flip!
Quick, Jim! A storm is starting ...

Jim has a good plan!

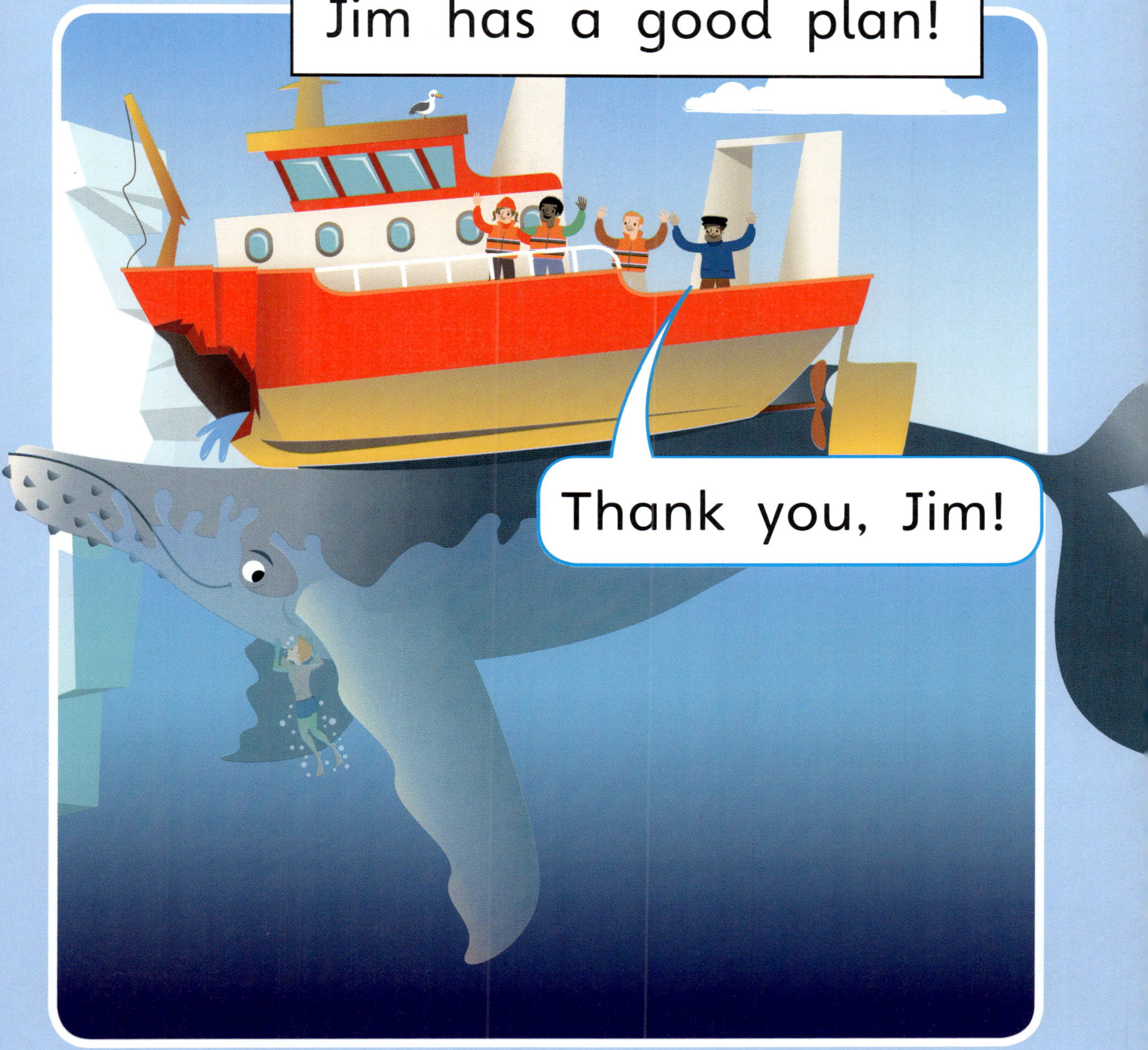

Eek! A shark is lurking in the surf!

Jim pops up!
Grrr!
You can not get me!

Jim darts up and down.
Flip!
He turns back.
Flip!
Jim is too quick for the shark!
Flip!

The shark spins.

The shark's tail is in a coil!

The shark can not swim!

Jim is a star!